Betty N. Barlow

EASIEST VIOLIN DUETS FOR CHRISTMAS

BOOK TWO

CONTENTS

G. SCHIRMER, Inc.

DISTRIBUTED BY
HAL•LEONARD®
CORPORATION
7777 W. BLUEMOUND RD. P.O. BOX 13819 MILWAUKEE, WI 53213

ED. 3213

EASIEST VIOLIN DUETS FOR CHRISTMAS
with Piano Accompaniment

Arrangements by
Betty M. Barlow

CZECHOSLOVAKIAN CAROL

AWAY IN A MANGER

Traditional

1st Violin

2nd Violin

Piano

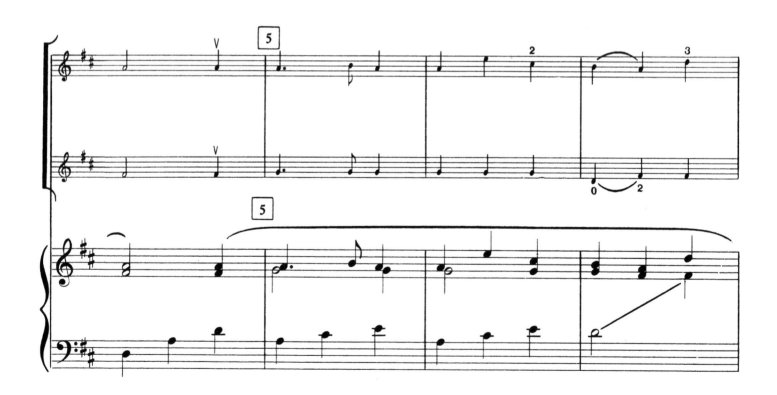

O THOU JOYFUL DAY

Sicilian Hymn

O COME, ALL YE FAITHFUL

John Reading

SILENT NIGHT

Franz Grüber

DECK THE HALLS

Welsh Air

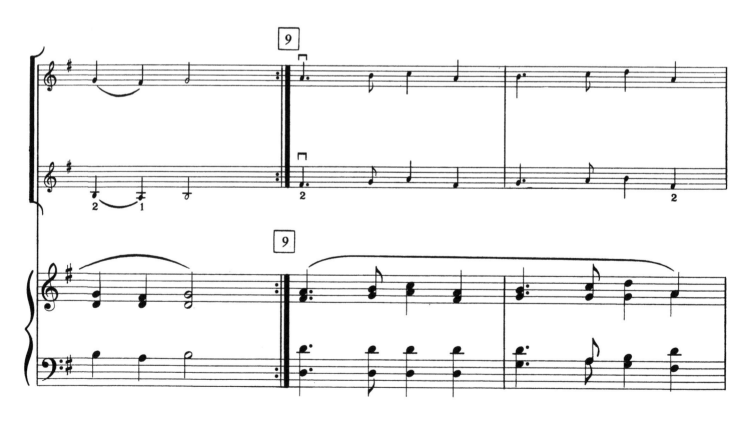

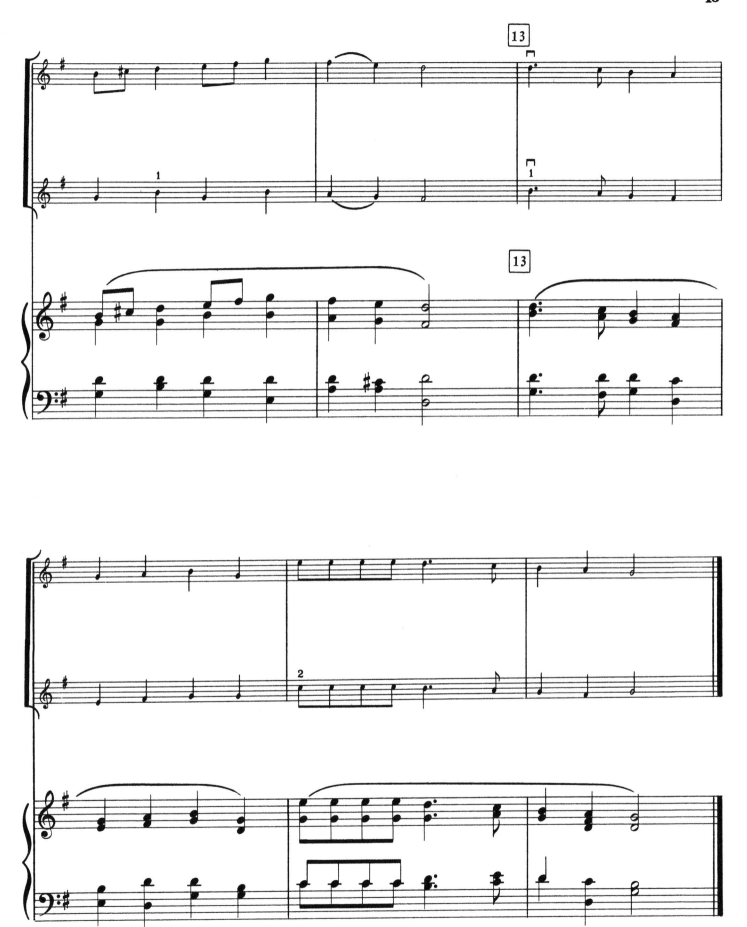

HARK! THE HERALD ANGELS SING

Felix Mendelssohn

ANGELS WE HAVE HEARD ON HIGH

French Carol

Violins

Betty N. Barlow
EASIEST VIOLIN DUETS FOR CHRISTMAS

BOOK TWO

CONTENTS

G. SCHIRMER, Inc.

DISTRIBUTED BY
HAL•LEONARD
CORPORATION
7777 W. BLUEMOUND RD. P.O. BOX 13819 MILWAUKEE, WI 53213

EASIEST VIOLIN DUETS FOR CHRISTMAS
with Piano Accompaniment

Arrangements by
Betty M. Barlow

CZECHOSLOVAKIAN CAROL

48166c

AWAY IN A MANGER

Traditional

O THOU JOYFUL DAY

Sicilian Hymn

O COME, ALL YE FAITHFUL

John Reading

SILENT NIGHT

Franz Grüber

1st Violin

2nd Violin

DECK THE HALLS

Welsh Air

HARK! THE HERALD ANGELS SING

Felix Mendelssohn

ANGELS WE HAVE HEARD ON HIGH

French Carol

JOY TO THE WORLD

George F. Handel

1st Violin

2nd Violin

THE FIRST NOEL

Traditional

O CHRISTMAS TREE

German Carol

WHILE SHEPHERDS WATCHED
THEIR FLOCKS BY NIGHT

George F. Handel

1st Violin

2nd Violin

GO TELL IT ON THE MOUNTAIN

Spiritual

IN DULCI JUBILO

Old German Melody

HERE WE COME A-WASSAILING

English Carol

Violins

Betty N. Barlow

EASIEST VIOLIN DUETS FOR CHRISTMAS

BOOK TWO

CONTENTS

G. SCHIRMER, Inc.

DISTRIBUTED BY

HAL•LEONARD®
CORPORATION

7777 W. BLUEMOUND RD. P.O. BOX 13819 MILWAUKEE, WI 53213

EASIEST VIOLIN DUETS FOR CHRISTMAS

with Piano Accompaniment

CZECHOSLOVAKIAN CAROL

Arrangements by
Betty M. Barlow

AWAY IN A MANGER

Traditional

O THOU JOYFUL DAY

Sicilian Hymn

O COME, ALL YE FAITHFUL

John Reading

SILENT NIGHT

Franz Grüber

1st Violin

2nd Violin

DECK THE HALLS

Welsh Air

HARK! THE HERALD ANGELS SING

Felix Mendelssohn

ANGELS WE HAVE HEARD ON HIGH

French Carol

JOY TO THE WORLD

George F. Handel

THE FIRST NOEL

Traditional

O CHRISTMAS TREE

German Carol

WHILE SHEPHERDS WATCHED
THEIR FLOCKS BY NIGHT

George F. Handel

1st Violin

2nd Violin

GO TELL IT ON THE MOUNTAIN

Spiritual

IN DULCI JUBILO

Old German Melody

HERE WE COME A-WASSAILING

English Carol

JOY TO THE WORLD

George F. Handel

1st Violin

2nd Violin

Piano

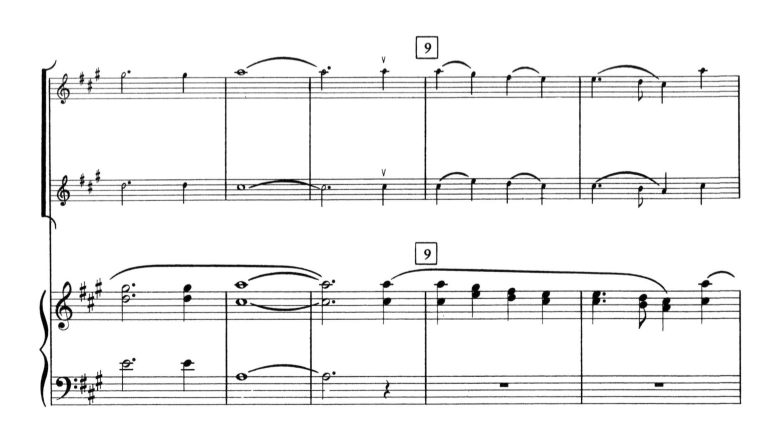

18

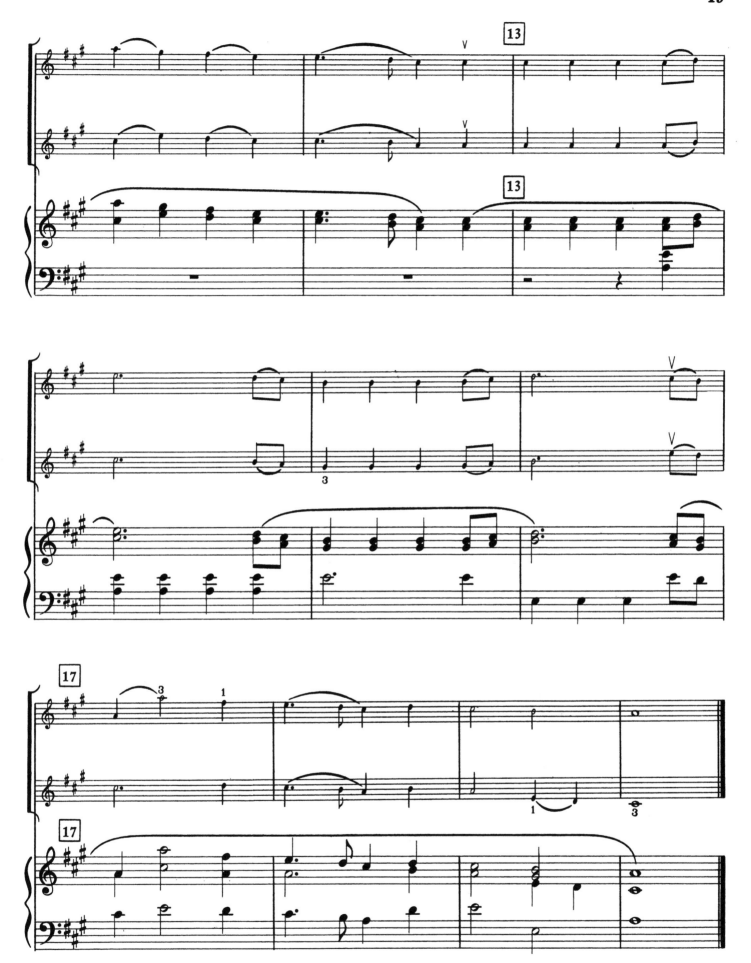

THE FIRST NOEL

Traditional

1st Violin

2nd Violin

Piano

O CHRISTMAS TREE

German Carol

WHILE SHEPHERDS WATCHED
THEIR FLOCKS BY NIGHT

George F. Handel

GO TELL IT ON THE MOUNTAIN

Spiritual

IN DULCI JUBILO

Old German Melody

HERE WE COME A-WASSAILING

English Carol

1st Violin

2nd Violin

Piano